?
HOW

HISTORY OPENS WINDOWS

Ancient
WEST AFRICAN
KINGDOMS

JANE SHUTER

Heinemann Library
Chicago, Illinois

Designed by Roslyn Broder
Printed and bound in the United States by Lake Book Manufacturing, Inc.

06 05 04 03 02
10 9 8 7 6 5 4 3 2 1

Library of Congress Cataloging-in-Publication Data
Shuter, Jane.
    Ancient West African kingdoms / Jane Shuter Heinemann.
       p. cm. — (History opens windows)
    Summary: Provides an overview of the culture and civilizations of the ancient West African Kingdoms of Mali, Ghana, and Songhai. Includes bibliographical references and index.
    ISBN: 1-4034-0255-8 (HC), 1-4034-0083-0 (Pbk.)
    1. Mali (Empire)—History—Juvenile literature. 2. Ghana (Empire)—History—Juvenile literature. 3. Songhai Empire—History—Juvenile literatrue. [1. Mali (Empire)—History. 2. Ghana (Empire)—History. 3. Songhai Empire—History. 4. Africa, West—History.] I. Title. II. Series.
    DT532 .S46 2002
    966.23—dc21
                                    2002000807

Acknowledgments
The author and publishers are grateful to the following for permission to reproduce copyright material:
p. 7 Werner Forman Archive/L. Entwistle Collection; p. 9 The Detroit Institute of Arts; p. 11 The University of Iowa Museum of Art, The Stanley Collection (1986.490); p. 12 Photograph by Franko Khoury/National Museum of African Art, Smithsonian Institution; p. 13 Giraudon/Art Resouce, NY; p. 16 Abbas/Magnum Photos, Inc.; pp. 17, 22, 23, 29 Wolfgang Kaehler; p. 18 Michael Kirtley/National Geographic Society Image Collection; p. 19 Mary Evans Picture Library; p. 24 The University of Iowa Museum of Art, The Stanley Collection (1986.451); p. 25 Werner Forman Archive/Private Collection, London; pp. 26, 30 Georg Gerster/Photo Researchers, Inc.; p. 28 Thomas A. Hale, Pennsylvania State University

Illustrations: p. 4 Eileen Mueller Neill; pp. 15, 21, 27 Juvenal "Marty" Martinez
Cover photograph courtesy of Franko Khoury/National Museum of African Art

Every effort has been made to contact copyright holders of any material reproduced in this book. Any omissions will be rectified in subsequent printings if notice is given to the publisher.

Some words are shown in bold, **like this.** You can find out what they mean by looking in the glossary.

Contents

Introduction

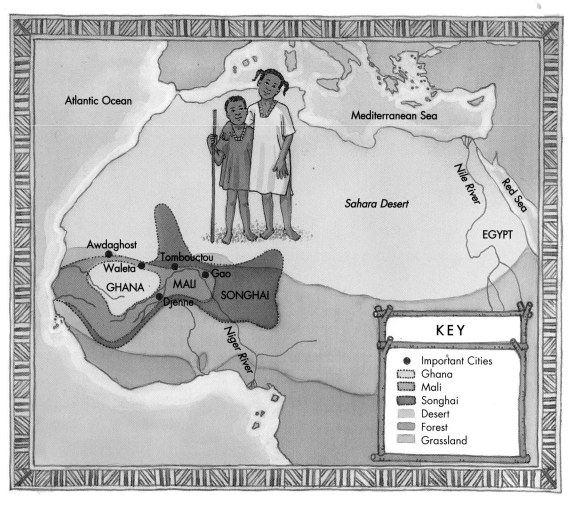

This map shows the kingdoms of Ghana, Mali, and Songhai, which ruled part of West Africa at different times between 700 and 1600.

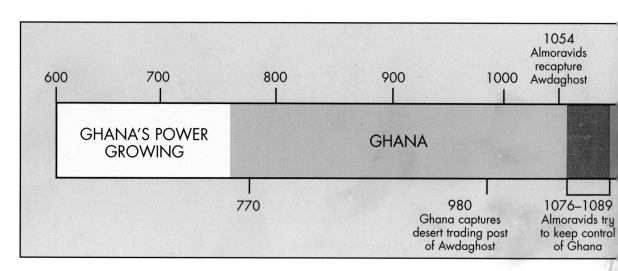

For hundreds of years, West Africa has been made up of different kingdoms. These kingdoms all have different languages and cultures. Their daily lives are very similar, because they are all affected by the same weather and landscape. So they all farm the same kinds of crops in the same kinds of ways. They live a mostly outdoor life.

Between 770 and 1591, three different kingdoms came to be the most important kingdoms in West Africa. They all became powerful because of trade with the kingdoms on the other side of the Sahara. They were the kingdoms of Ghana, Mali, and Songhai. These kingdoms all seemed to fall apart for similar reasons. They grew too much and their rulers could not keep control. Also, they used their power to make trade unfair for the people they traded with. Both Ghana and Songhai were invaded by angry groups from the other side of the desert.

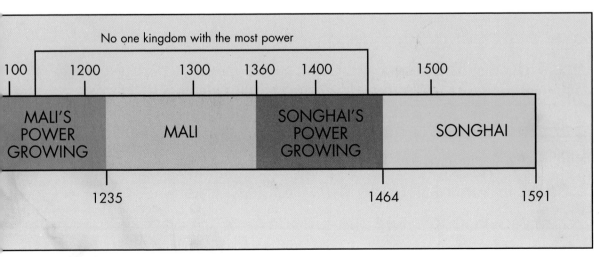

Ghana

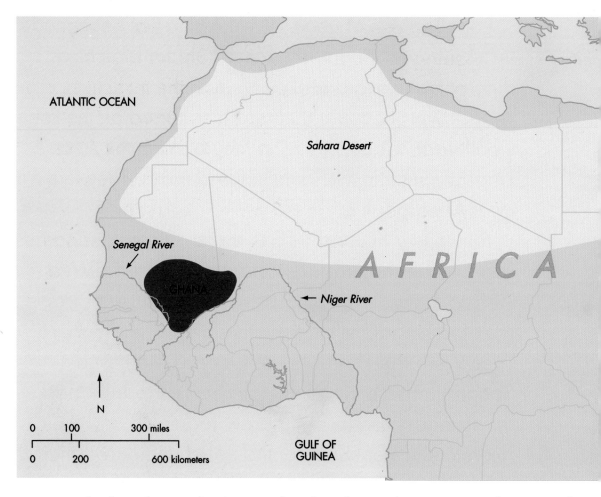

People lived in Ghana as far back as the year 300. They were one of many groups living in West Africa. Ghana had a huge advantage over the other groups because it was on the edge of the Sahara. By about 770, the kings of Ghana had control of the trade routes to the Sahara. Anyone who wanted to trade with the people of the desert had to pay a tax to the king of Ghana for using these routes. This is when most people see the kingdom of Ghana as beginning.

This map show. the kingdom of Ghana at its largest, in about 1000.

The desert trade was based on a system of being fair. But the kings of Ghana became greedy. When they took over the trading post of Awdaghost, which had been controlled by the North African Almoravids, the kings of Ghana became too powerful. In about 1054, the Almoravids attacked and took Awdaghost back.

Over the next twenty years, they took over more and more of Ghana. It was hard for them to control the kingdom because they were not West Africans themselves. Ghana soon broke up into several small kingdoms. The people of one of these kingdoms, Keita, eventually grew strong and set up the kingdom of Mali.

The Akan people began to settle in Ghana just after the kingdom broke up. This clay head probably represents an Akan king.

7

Mali

The people of Keita, one of the kingdoms that formed when Ghana broke up, began the kingdom of Mali. So there is a clear link of people and location between the kingdoms of Ghana and Mali. The kingdom of Mali started with the rule of King Sundiata, who became king in 1235. Sundiata had a strong army, which he used to take over nearby kingdoms. Soon, Mali grew bigger and took control of the trade routes across the Sahara. Control of the trade routes made Mali richer and more powerful.

This map shows the kingdom of Mali at its largest, in about 1300.

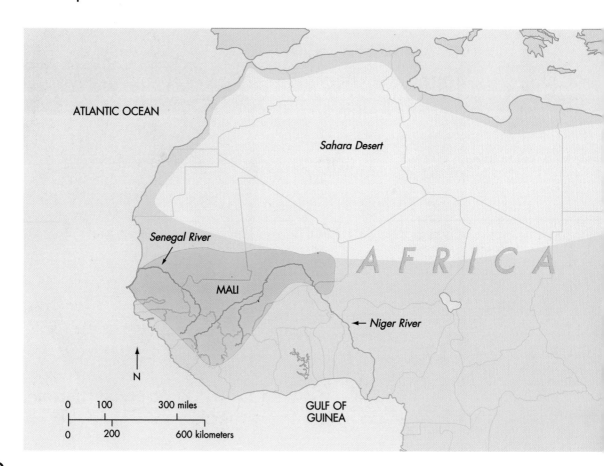

ATLANTIC OCEAN

Sahara Desert

Senegal River

MALI

A F R I C A

Niger River

N

| 0 | 100 | 300 miles |

| 0 | 200 | 600 kilometers |

GULF OF GUINEA

By 1300, the kingdom of Mali was more than twice the size of the old kingdom of Ghana and had about twice as many people living in it. It was rich, peaceful, and had good rulers. But Mali had become too big. It had taken over too many different kingdoms.

These kingdoms all had different cultures, different languages, and their own royal families. They were not always happy to accept the king of Mali as their ruler. These people were quick to take advantage of a long argument over who should be the next king. Their kingdoms broke away and the kingdom of Mali collapsed. One of these "breakaway" kingdoms was the kingdom of Songhai.

*Many **terra-cotta** figurines have been found in the city of Djenne. This figure is probably a portrait of a man who had died.*

Songhai

The kingdom of Songhai had been part of the kingdom of Mali. Songhai was on the Niger River, and the skills of its sailors were very useful for trade in Mali. Songhai was one of the first kingdoms to break away as Mali kings lost control.

Starting in 1464, the kings of Songhai steadily took over lands that had once been part of the kingdom of Mali. By 1492, when the warrior king Sonni Ali died, Songhai controlled a huge kingdom and the important trade routes across the Sahara.

This map shows the kingdom of Songhai at its largest, in about 1490.

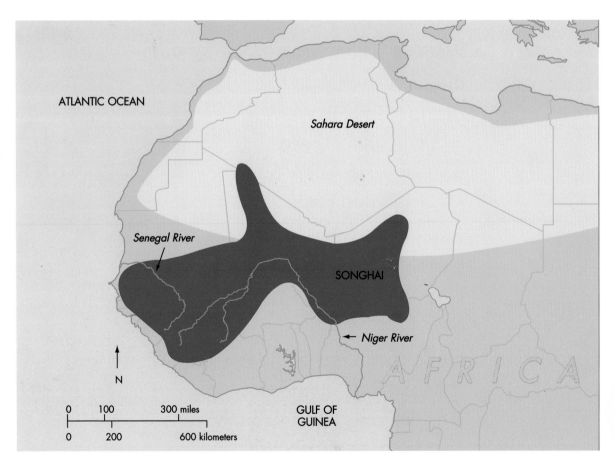

ATLANTIC OCEAN

Sahara Desert

Senegal River

SONGHAI

← Niger River

N

AFRICA

0   100   300 miles

0   200   600 kilometers

GULF OF GUINEA

Songhai was the biggest of the three great West African kingdoms. This made it hard to control. Askia Muhammad, who ruled after Sonni Ali, also made the mistake of taking over the salt trade as well as the gold trade. The desert people had always controlled the salt trade, which kept trade fair between the two groups. Now Songhai had too much power in trade, too.

In 1528, Askia Muhammad's sons took over Songhai from their father. There were quarrels over who should rule. The kingdom began to break up. In 1591, the desert people of Morocco invaded and Songhai fell apart.

This clay figurine from Djenne shows two women embracing. ***Archaeologists*** *think they are mourning the death of their husband.*

How Were They Ruled?

All of the West African kingdoms were ruled by kings who came from royal families. Many of them were so powerful that they were seen almost as gods. Different kingdoms had different rules about who should take over. In some places, sons took over from their fathers. In others, children of the king's sister took over.

Many times it was not clear who was the right person to take over. So it was easy for arguments to break out over who the next ruler should be.

West African rulers were often shown on horseback. This figurine shows Sundiata Keita, the "Lion King of Mali."

This Spanish map of North Africa shows a West African king named Mansa Musa receiving a trader. Mansa Musa is dressed in blue and wears a crown.

Rulers lived in their palaces, away from the people. So other people ran the country for them. Most West African kings had **officials** of different levels of importance working for them. The officials enforced laws, collected taxes, and made sure that things ran smoothly. Songhai grew so large that it was split into twelve separate districts. Each had its own governor and officials. Ghana, Mali, and Songhai all had large armies to guard the trade routes and to keep control of the kingdom.

Trade

Trade was a very important part of life in West Africa. Ghana, Mali, and Songhai all became powerful mainly by controlling the trade with the groups of people who used the trade routes across the Sahara. Each group traded a variety of **goods.** However, salt and gold were the most important trade goods.

The West African kingdoms had a lot of gold, while the desert people controlled areas where salt could be mined. Traders also swapped copper, dried fruit, cowrie shells, and **slaves.**

The earliest traders did not meet each other to swap their goods. Instead, they used a system called "silent trade." Silent trade was an easy way for people who did not speak the same language to exchange goods. Later, traders met at **oases** or at trading points set up along rivers to trade. They still swapped goods instead of using money.

The silent trade system was very important to the people of North and West Africa. This diagram shows how it worked.

Desert traders bring
salt, spices, and other
goods they want to
trade to a desert oasis.

They lay out the goods, beat
the drums to call the West
African traders, then leave.

The West African traders decide
how much gold they want to give
for the salt and spices. They put the
gold next to the things they want.
They beat the drums and leave.

The desert traders return. If they
think the swap is fair, they take
the gold and go. If not, they leave
it, and bang the drums again.

The West Africans come back. If the
gold has gone, they take the goods
left behind. If the gold is still there,
they decide if they will give more. If
so, they add it and beat the drums
again. This goes on until everyone
has done all the trading they want.

15

Religion

The earliest West Africans believed in a powerful "creator god" who made the world but did not interfere in people's lives. They also believed in **spirits** that controlled nature and did interfere in daily life. People prayed or made **offerings** to these spirits to keep them happy. They believed their dead relatives could talk to these spirits in the spirit world, so they had to keep their relatives happy, too.

Some people, called **diviners,** were said to have strong links to the spirit world. They told people, or even whole villages, what kind of offerings they had to give and what **rituals** they had to do. Most rituals involved dancing and singing, and some of them took several days.

The Dogon people of Mali still worship their gods with masked dances, just like their ancestors did.

Many of the North African people who traded with the West Africans were **Muslims.** As silent trade moved on to personal trade, they brought their religious ideas with them. The kings of Mali became Muslims. They built Muslim **temples,** called **mosques,** in their cities. These cities became centers of Muslim religion and learning. One city, Tombouctou, was famous for its **universities.**

While the kings and their **courts** changed their religion, most of their people did not. In the countryside, ordinary people still kept their old beliefs. They were much slower to change.

The mosque in Djenne, Mali, was built out of mud bricks in the traditional style.

Cities

Most West Africans lived in large family groups in farming settlements. Starting in about 1000, cities began to grow where the kings lived with their families and **officials.** The cities became important as trading places. At first, only local people traded in the cities. Later, foreign traders came there too.

The king lived in his palace buildings, in a separate part of the city from everyone else. From time to time he allowed people to come to his palace and ask for favors. Most of the time his officials enforced the laws. The king did not have to do it himself.

West African cities were important centers for crafts and trade. Skilled craft workers, like this potter, still use many of the same methods today.

The city of Tombouctou became an important meeting place for people from all over West Africa. They traded not just goods, but ideas too.

Djenne was one of the earliest cities. By the year 1000, there were about 10,000 people living there. (London, one of the biggest European cities, had 40,000 people living in it at the time.) Most of the people living in the city were craft workers. Each type of craft worker lived in a separate part of the city.

Tombouctou was founded at about the same time. Under the rule of the Songhai kings, it grew in size until there were thousands of people living there. It had a royal palace, many **mosques,** busy markets, and a famous **university.**

Houses

Most people did not live in cities. They lived in villages in large family groups. Some villages were very small, with fewer than fifty people living in them. Others were much larger. Villages had to be big enough that all the people living there could make and grow everything the village needed.

Each village had a central circular **plaza,** with "compounds" leading off from it. A compound was a group of huts around a central courtyard where much of the work was done. The chief of a village was expected to marry several women. He had a compound for each wife and at least one compound for his animals. Cattle were a sign of wealth, so a chief would hope to have lots of cattle. Less important people might only have one compound for everyone in the family and their animals.

This illustration shows a group of typical West African compounds.

Animals were brought into a fenced compound at night to keep them safe from wild animals that might want to eat them.

Grain was sometimes stored in raised storage bins that looked like small huts.

The doors of houses did not come all the way to the ground. A raised doorway made it harder for small animals to get in.

Each compound had its own fences.

Food and Farming

West African farmers grew millet, sorghum, nuts, rice, and cotton. Farmers used simple hand tools, such as digging sticks and sickles, to dig the soil and **harvest** the crops. Because of the heat, the crops needed careful watering.

Farmers kept chickens for eggs and meat. They kept cows and goats for milk and meat. Merchants and important people kept horses and camels for transportation. The West African people used every part of the animals when they were killed. Feathers were used on clothes and masks. The fat was used for cooking, making candles, and softening dry skin.

The men of this village in Senegal work together to prepare freshly harvested grain, just as the ancient West Africans did.

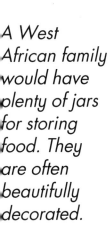
A West African family would have plenty of jars for storing food. They are often beautifully decorated.

Millet was the most important crop. It was ground up to make porridge or ground even finer to make flour for bread. It was also used to make a weak beer. Most people only ate meat on special occasions. Almost everyone drank milk or beer, especially if they did not live close to a source of fresh water.

The women of the family cooked over an open fire, usually outside. In the rainy season they cooked in a special kitchen hut. They did not cook in their homes because they were afraid of starting a fire. Each village had at least one large bread oven where the women baked bread.

Families

West Africans lived in large family groups. Marriages were arranged by the families. The wife usually went to live with her husband's family. The husband's family paid a "bride price," usually cattle or cloth, for the wife. The amount of the bride price depended on how rich the families were.

Everyone living in the village was expected to help everyone else. In each compound, the children called all old women "grandmother" and all old men "grandfather." They all called each other "brother" and "sister."

*Family and ancestors are very important in West Africa. Figures like this are buried in graves and provide a link between the living and the **spirit** of the person who has died.*

Men and women lived very separate lives. Men worked together, joked together, and ate together. The women worked and ate with the children. There were special **ceremonies** for when a boy was old enough to stop living like a child, with the women and children, and join the men. Boys learned the same trade as their fathers and uncles, and they had to learn the secret **rituals** of songs and dances that each trade had. Girls learned how to run a home.

Everyone joined together for weddings, funerals, and rituals held at special times, such as **harvest** time. Some of these **festivals** lasted for days, with a lot of singing, dancing, eating, and drinking.

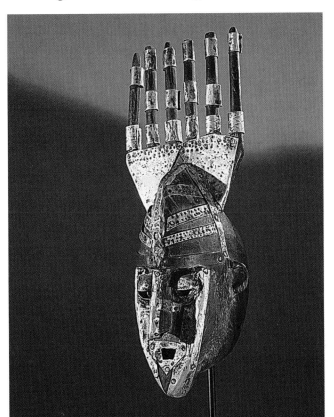

Masks play an important part in many ceremonies in West Africa.

Clothes

The weather in West Africa was very hot, even during the rainy season, but the nights could get cold sometimes. Most of the time, though, people did not need to wear clothes to keep warm. The earliest West Africans went naked, with maybe an animal skin as a cloak in the coldest weather.

Later, clothes came to be a way of showing importance and wealth. There was a rule in some kingdoms that only the king could wear sandals. Unlike everyone else, he was too important to have his feet touch the ground. People, especially in the cities, began to wear more clothes as they met people from other cultures who wore more clothes, such as the **Muslim** traders from the north.

Gold jewelry was one of the ways that people could show their wealth and importance. This woman is wearing huge gold earrings.

Because the
weather in West
Africa is so
warm, most
people just wore
a simple apron
and no shoes.
The woman is
carrying a baby
in a cloth sling.

When West African
traders began to meet
traders from North Africa
face to face, many of
them began to dress in
the same way. This West
African trader is wearing
a long robe like those
worn by traders from
across the Sahara.

A king would
wear sandals,
an elegant tunic,
and a skullcap.
His servant wears
a plain apron
and carries a
shade to protect
the king from
the sun.

Writing and Storytelling

The people of West Africa had a spoken language, but they did not believe in writing things down at first. For many years they passed on stories and knowledge **orally.**

Some people enjoyed riddles and **proverbs** that anyone could tell. But there were storytellers called **griots,** whose job it was to remember and pass on the important stories of each group of people. Often they would tell their stories to music, carrying a drum or a stringed instrument to play the tunes. They told the stories at **rituals,** often with the help of other people acting out the story with masks and dancing.

Griots are still an important part of West African culture. A female griot is called a griotte.

This book was found in Tombouctou. It is written in Arabic, the main language of many Muslims.

While the West Africans did not have a tradition of writing things down, the North African **Muslims** they traded with did. Muslim travelers wrote the only descriptions we have of Tombouctou and Djenne at the time. They also wrote down the names of the rulers and their laws and customs.

As West African rulers became Muslim, they needed to read the **Qur'an** and obey Muslim laws. To do this, they had to learn to read and write. Teachers came to the cities from North Africa, and schools and **universities** sprang up.

29

Modern West Africa

Some of the photographs in this book show modern West Africa. This is because the people there do many things in the same way as their ancestors from the old kingdoms of Ghana, Mali, and Songhai. Farmers grow similar crops in similar ways. Homes in the countryside are still built using similar materials to cope with a similar climate. Storytellers and **griots** still tell the same stories.

Not everything is unchanged. The cities have changed the most. They have electricity, cars, telephones, and other modern inventions.

Huge slabs of salt are for sale at a large market. Salt is still one of the main trade goods in West Africa.

Glossary

archaeologist person who studies people and objects from the past

ceremony set of acts with religious meaning

court king or queen and the people who advise them

diviner person who tells ordinary people how to please the gods

festival time of celebration with special events and entertainment

goods things made or grown to trade or swap

griot West African storyteller and musician

harvest season when crops are gathered; or, to gather a crop

mosque Muslim temple

Muslim member of a religious group that follows the teachings of the prophet Muhammed

oasis green spot in the middle of a desert. The plural is **oases.**

offering something given to a god

official person who runs a country for the ruler

oral spoken, not written

plaza large open square in the center of a city or town

proverb wise saying

Qur'an Muslim holy book

ritual ceremony that is done the same way every time

slave someone who belongs to someone else and is forced to work without pay

spirit being that has life but cannot be seen

temple building for religious worship

terra-cotta baked clay that can be used to make bricks, pots, sculptures, and many other things

university high-level school that gives degrees in many fields

More Books to Read

Brownlie, Alison. *West Africa.* Austin, Tex.: Raintree Steck-Vaughn Publishers, 1999.

Nelson, Julie. *Great African Kingdoms.* Austin, Tex.: Raintree Steck-Vaughn Publishers, 2001.

Wisniewski, David. *Sundiata: Lion King of Mali.* New York: Clarion Books, 1999.

Index